D0930692

Mini Artist

Making Puppets

Toby Reynolds

WINDMILL
BOOKS
New York

Published in 2016 by **Windmill Books**, an Imprint of Rosen Publishing
29 East 21st Street, New York, NY 10010

Puppets made by Fiona Gowen.

Images on pages 4 and 5 © shutterstock.com

Cataloging-in-Publication Data
Reynolds, Toby.
Making puppets / by Toby Reynolds.
p. cm. — (Mini artists)
Includes index.
ISBN 978-1-4777-5674-4 (pbk.)
ISBN 978-1-4777-5673-7 (6 pack)
ISBN 978-1-4777-5576-1 (library binding)
1. Puppet making — Juvenile literature. I. Reynolds, Toby. II. Title.
TT174.7 R434 2016
745.592—d23

Manufactured in the United States of America

CPSIA Compliance Information: Batch # WS15WM: For Further Information contact Rosen Publishing, New York, New York at 1-800-237-9932

Contents

4

Getting Started

The projects in this book use lots of art materials that
you will already have at home. Any missing materials
can be found in art shops and stationery stores.

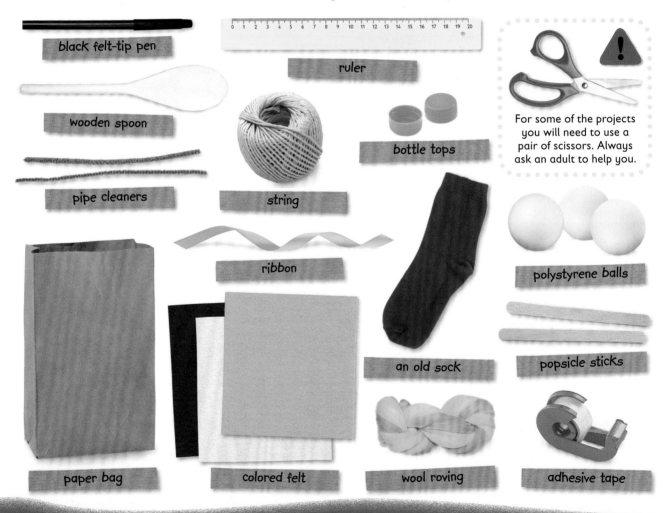

black felt-tip pen

ruler

wooden spoon

bottle tops

For some of the projects
you will need to use a
pair of scissors. Always
ask an adult to help you.

pipe cleaners

string

polystyrene balls

ribbon

popsicle sticks

an old sock

paper bag

colored felt

wool roving

adhesive tape

old pencils

wool

paper cups

empty box

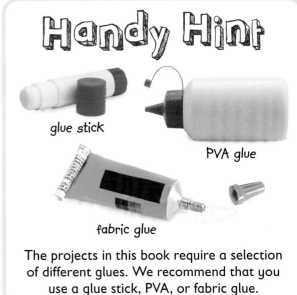

Handy Hint

glue stick

PVA glue

fabric glue

The projects in this book require a selection of different glues. We recommend that you use a glue stick, PVA, or fabric glue.

Here is a selection of paper and card stock you can use to complete the puppet projects.

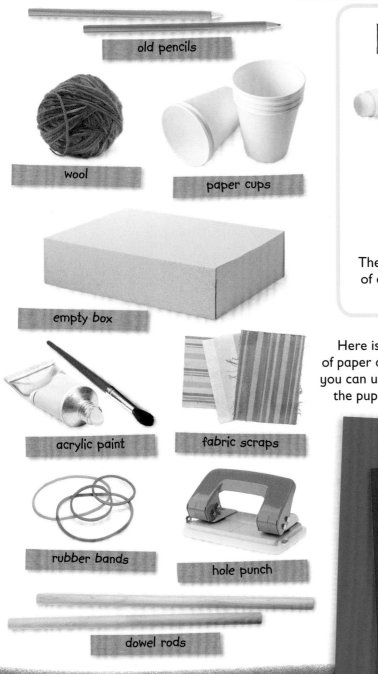

acrylic paint

fabric scraps

rubber bands

hole punch

dowel rods

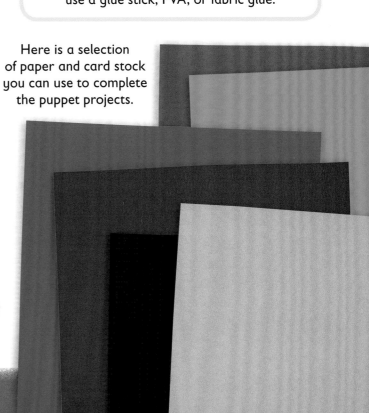

Spoon Puppet

To make this puppet you will need a wooden spoon, wool, fabric, a felt-tip pen, ribbon, and fabric glue.

1 Start by cutting lengths of wool to the same size. Tie the wool together in three evenly-spaced places.

2 Put some fabric glue onto the top of your wooden spoon and stick the wool in place to look like hair.

3 Now take your black felt-tip pen and draw some eyes and a mouth directly onto the wooden spoon.

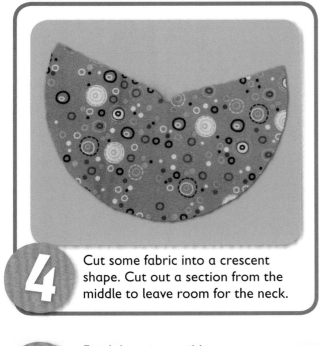

4 Cut some fabric into a crescent shape. Cut out a section from the middle to leave room for the neck.

5 Use fabric glue to attach the dress to your spoon. Glue the dress flaps together at the back of the spoon.

6 Finish by tying a ribbon to her neck and a bow in your puppet's hair. Now you can make some friends for her.

Fish Sock Puppet

To make this fun sock puppet you will need an old sock, a selection of colored felt, and fabric glue.

1 Start your puppet by finding an old sock. Make sure that your sock does not have any holes or rips in it.

2 Cut an oval shape from pale felt and use fabric glue to stick it firmly into position on the toe end of your sock.

3 Now you can cut two fin shapes from colored felt. These can be glued to either side of your sock.

4 Turn your puppet over and glue two white felt ovals for eyes. Cut smaller pieces of black felt and glue on top.

5 Cut two more fin shapes from the colored felt. Glue them into position on your puppet as shown.

6 Finish your puppet by cutting two tail shapes and gluing them to the end of your sock.

10

Paper Cup Mermaid

You will need a paper cup, a hole punch, card stock, pipe cleaners, PVA glue, a pencil, string, and paints.

1 Start your puppet by painting a face onto an upside-down paper cup. Ask an adult to cut a hole in the top.

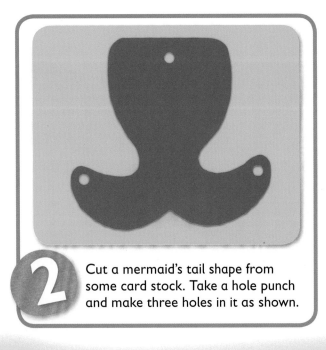

2 Cut a mermaid's tail shape from some card stock. Take a hole punch and make three holes in it as shown.

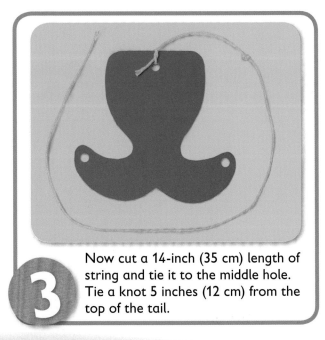

3 Now cut a 14-inch (35 cm) length of string and tie it to the middle hole. Tie a knot 5 inches (12 cm) from the top of the tail.

4 Now thread the string through the hole in the top of the cup. Tie the end of the string to an old pencil.

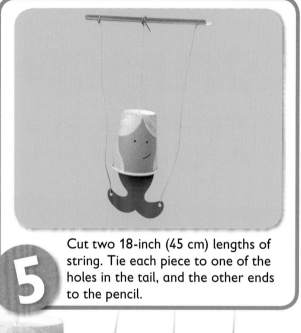

5 Cut two 18-inch (45 cm) lengths of string. Tie each piece to one of the holes in the tail, and the other ends to the pencil.

6 Ask an adult to make holes in either side of the cup. Thread some pipe cleaners through for arms.

Dragon Puppet

For this puppet you will need popsicle sticks, paper, card stock, a felt-tip pen, scissors, and a glue stick.

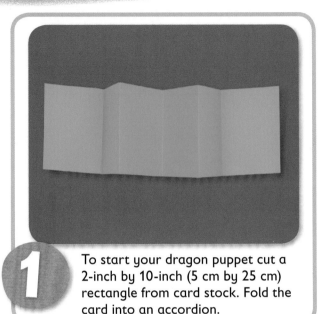

1 To start your dragon puppet cut a 2-inch by 10-inch (5 cm by 25 cm) rectangle from card stock. Fold the card into an accordion.

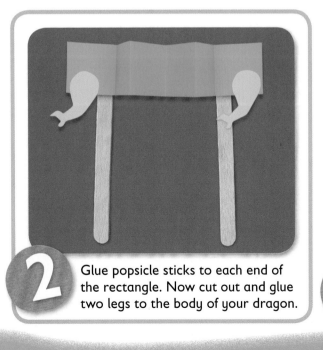

2 Glue popsicle sticks to each end of the rectangle. Now cut out and glue two legs to the body of your dragon.

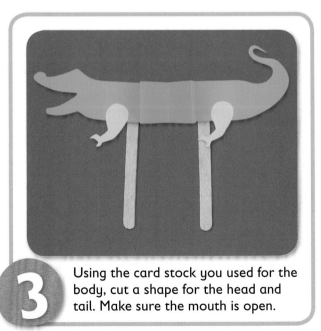

3 Using the card stock you used for the body, cut a shape for the head and tail. Make sure the mouth is open.

4 Add a white paper eye. Draw a black dot on the eye and one for a nostril. Add some white paper teeth.

5 Glue some colorful paper spikes all the way along the dragon's back and then add a large horn and tail spike.

6 Finish your dragon by gluing paper flames coming out of the mouth. Add some paper scales to the body.

14

Box Monster

To make this puppet you will need a cardboard box, paints, PVA glue, card stock, bottle tops, and wool roving.

1 First paint the box. When it is dry, ask an adult to cut halfway around the box, leaving the bottom uncut.

2 Fold your cardboard box into two halves. This will form the moving mouth part of your monster puppet.

3 Use PVA glue to attach two bottle tops for eyes. Glue white and black card stock circles for each of the eyes.

4 Now you can add the hair. Cut some wool roving and glue it sticking up behind the eyes of your monster.

5 Glue two black card stock circles onto the monster to make the nostrils. Glue on white card stock triangles for fangs.

6

Finally glue a long forked tongue into the mouth. Now you can make your monster a friend.

16

Bear Puppet

To make this hand puppet you will need a selection of colored felt, scissors, and fabric glue.

1 You can start this puppet project by cutting the basic bear shape from two large pieces of brown felt.

2 Carefully stick the edges of your two puppet pieces together. Remember not to glue the bottom edge!

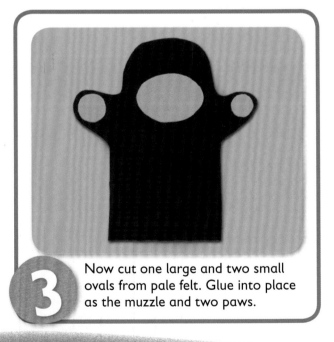

3 Now cut one large and two small ovals from pale felt. Glue into place as the muzzle and two paws.

4 To make the ears, cut two circles of pale felt and two larger circles of brown felt. Glue these into place.

5 Glue on white circles for eyes, then smaller black circles inside. Use your black felt for the nose and mouth.

6 You can now make more bear puppets. Try to give them different expressions on their faces.

Peekaboo Puppet

For this puppet you will need a rubber band, a felt-tip pen, a dowel rod, card stock, scissors, glue, tape and felt.

1 Start this puppet by taping together the card stock into a cone. The dowel should be able to slide in and out of this cone.

2 Make a felt cone and glue one end to the card stock, attach the other end to the dowel with a rubber band.

3 Now use card stock to make the face of your puppet. Remember to add details for the eyes, nose and mouth.

4 Use sticky tape to attach the face of the puppet to the top of the dowel. You can tape over the rubber band.

5 Now you can make a cover for the card cone. Use scissors to snip into the edge so that it looks like grass.

6 There are many different types of peekaboo puppets you can make.

Paper Bag Owl

To make this funny owl you will need a brown paper bag, colored card stock, scissors, and a glue stick.

1 Take a clean brown bag and turn it upside down. Cut a heart shape out of brown card stock and glue onto the top.

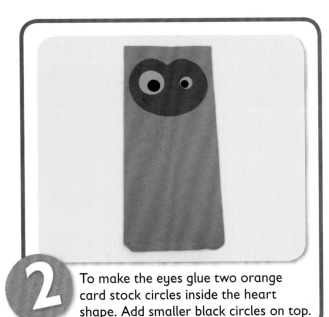

2 To make the eyes glue two orange card stock circles inside the heart shape. Add smaller black circles on top.

3 Use the brown card stock again and cut out some feather shapes. Glue these on either side of the owl's head.

4 Cut out two dark brown wings and two smaller pale wing shapes. Glue these onto the back of the bag.

5 Use gray card stock to make a beak and claws. Glue the beak to the face and the claws to the bottom of the bag.

6 Now you can make a family of owl puppets. All sorts of puppets can be made using paper bags.

Finger Puppets

For this puppet you will need felt, wool, scissors, a felt-tip pen, fabric glue, paints, and a polystyrene ball.

1 Wrap a rectangle of felt around your finger to check the size. Glue the overlap to form a cylinder.

2 Cut thin strips of felt for arms and glue these to the body. At the end of each arm glue a felt hand in place.

3 Now paint a polystyrene ball with a skin-colored paint. When dry, glue it on top of the puppet's body.

4 To decorate your puppet's head cut lengths of wool and glue them to the polystyrene ball for hair and a beard.

5 Create a hat for your finger puppet from black felt and glue on. Now use a felt-tip pen to draw on the face.

6 Follow the steps to make other fun finger puppets. Try making some animals as well as people!

Glossary

accordion a portable keyboard wind instrument in which the wind is forced past free reeds by means of a hand-operated bellows

crescent a curved shape, such as the moon when less than half of it is visible

felt a cloth made of wool and fur often mixed with natural or artificial fibers

muzzle the snout of an animal, consisting of the jaws and nose

nostril an opening through which an animal breathes; usually part of the nose

polystyrene a rigid plastic used in foams and molded products

Index

Further Reading

Cook, Trevor, and Sally Henry. *Making Puppets*. New York: PowerKids Press, 2011.

Skillcorn, Helen. *Spooky Crafts*. New York: Gareth Stevens, 2010.

Websites

For web resources related to the subject of this book, go to: **www.windmillbooks.com/weblinks** and select this book's title.